Ralph

VAUGHAN WILLIAMS

A SEA SYMPHONY

Symphony No. 1

(1909)

Vocal Score

Klavierauszug

PETRUCCI LIBRARY PRESS

CONTENTS

Duration: ca.70 minutes

First performance: October 12, 1910
Leeds Triennial Festival, Leeds Town Hall
Cicely Gleeson-White (soprano), Campbell McInnes (baritone)
Festival Chorus, Orchestra
Ralph Vaughan Williams (conductor)

ISMN: 979-0-58021-352-5

This score is a slightly modified unabridged reprint of the score
issued in 1909, 1918 by Breitkopf & Härtel (later Stainer & Bell), London.
The score has been scaled to fit the present format.

A SEA SYMPHONY.

For Soprano and Baritone Soli, Chorus and Orchestra.

WALT WHITMAN. R. VAUGHAN WILLIAMS.

Nº 1. A Song for all seas, all ships.

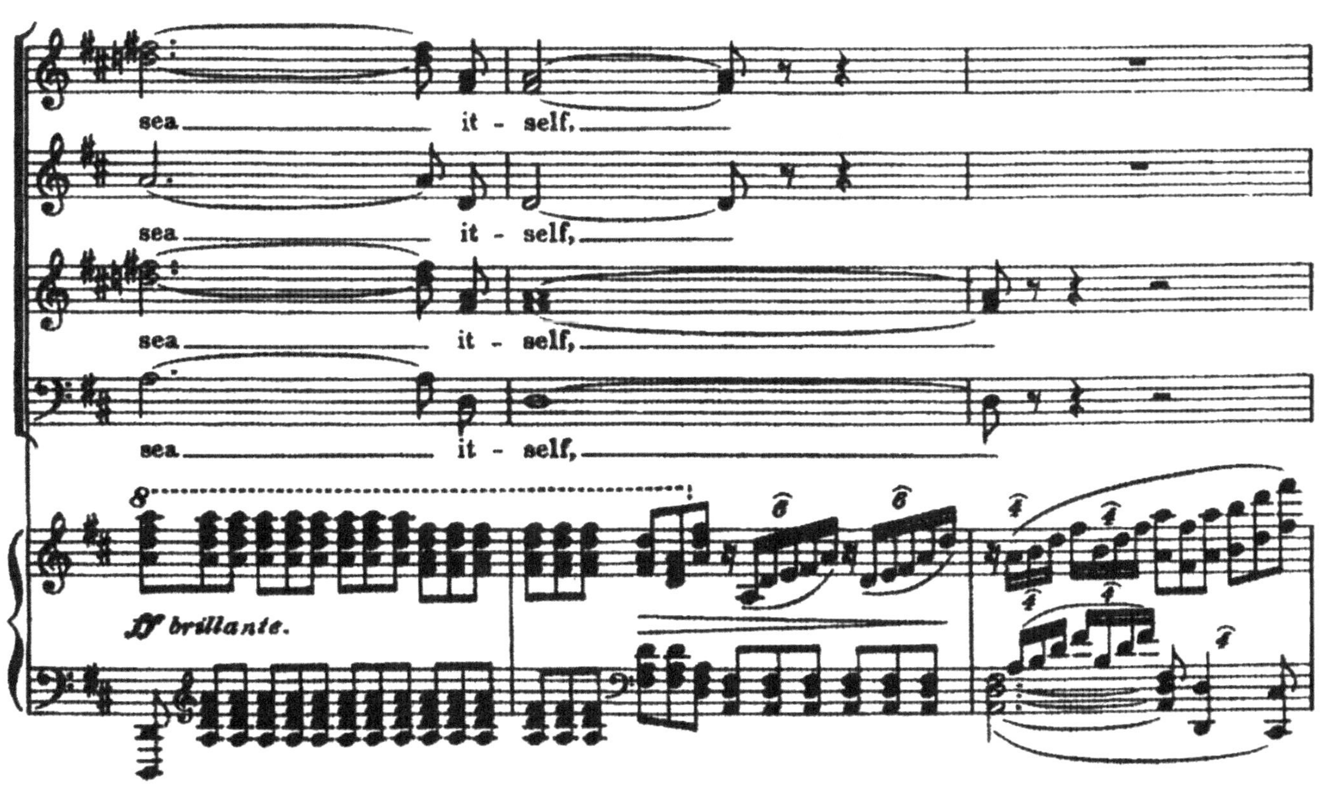

poco f ma dolce
And on its
poco f ma dolce
And on its
f cantabile
m. d.
largamente
m. d.
poco f ma dolce
And on its lim-it-less, heav-ing breast the
lim-it-less, heav-ing breast, the ships; See, where their
poco f ma dolce
And on its lim-it-less, heav-ing breast the
lim-it-less, heav-ing breast, the ships; See, where their
ships; See, where their white sails, bel-ly-ing in the
white sails, bel-ly-ing in the wind, see, where their
ships; See, where their white sails, see, where their white
white sails, bel-ly-ing in the wind, where their white

A
wind, see where their white sails see
white sails, their white sails speckle the
sails, their white sails, bel-ly-ing in the wind, see
sails, See, see where their white sails, speckle the
A
green and blue, See, the
green and blue, See, the
see their white sails
green and blue,
f
Poco animando.
ff
steam - ers com - ing and go - ing,
steam - ers com - ing and go - ing,
See, the steam - ers com - ing and
See, the steam - ers com - ing and
marcato

steam - - - - - ing
steam - - - - - ing
go - ing,
steam - -
go - ing,
steam - -
in or out of port,
in or out of port,
- - - - - ing
in or out of port,
- - - - - ing
in or out of port,
marcato
B
See,
See,
See,
See,
See,
See,
marcato

accel.
dusk - y and un-du-lat-ing, See,
accel.
dusk - y and un du-lat-ing, See,
accel.
dusk - y and un-du-lat-ing, See,
accel.
dusk - y and un-du-lat-ing, See,
accel.
C
See, the long pen-nants of smoke.
See, the long pen-nants of smoke.
See, the long pen-nants of smoke.
See, the long pen-nants of smoke.
C
fff
Più mosso.
p

Tempo I.
Be - hold, the
Be - hold, the
Be - hold, the
Be - hold, the
Tempo I.
D Largamente.
sea it - self,
sea it - self,
sea it - self,
sea it - self,
D Largamente.
And on its lim-it-less heav - - ing
And on its lim-it-less heav - - ing
And on its lim-it-less heav - - ing
And on its lim-it-less heav - - ing

breast,
the
ships.
breast,
the
ships.
breast,
the
ships.
breast,
the
ships.
dim.
E
Molto tranquillo.
p
Allegro. ♩= 126
p
simile

F
BARITONE SOLO.
To-day a rude brief re-ci-ta-tive, Of ships sail-ing the seas, each with its special flag or ship-sig-nal,
p
G
simile
Of un-named he-roes in the ships of waves spread-ing and spread-ing far as the eye can reach,
f marcato
Of dash-ing spray, and the winds pip-ing and blow-ing,
p
f
simile
p
simile

CHORUS.
H
ff
Of dash-ing spray and the winds pip - ing and
Of dash - ing spray and the winds pip - ing and
Of dash-ing spray and the winds pip - ing and
Of dash - ing spray and the winds pip-ing and
f marcato
simile
blow - ing,
blow - ing,
blow - ing,
blow - ing,
f marcato
simile
To -
To -
To -
To -
tr

-day a rude brief re-ci-ta - tive,
Of ships sail-ing the seas,
ff marcato
each with its spe-cial flag or ship - sig-nal,
Of un - named he-roes in the
ships of waves spread - ing
ships of waves spread-ing far
ships of waves spread - ing
ships of waves spread - ing, spread-ing far
mf
marcato

ff
K
far — as the eye can reach,
as — the — eye can reach,
far — as the eye can reach,
as — the — eye can reach,
ff marc.
Of dash-ing spray, and the winds pip-ing and blow - - ing,
Of dash-ing spray, and the winds pip-ing and blow - - ing,
Of dash-ing spray, and the winds pip-ing and blow - - ing,
Of dash-ing spray. and the winds pip-ing and blow - - ing,

of dashing spray,
of dashing spray,
of dashing spray,
of dashing spray,
marcato
L
and the winds piping and blow - - - - ing.
and the winds piping and blow - - - - ing.
and the winds piping and blow - - - - ing.
and the winds piping and blow - - - - ing.
L

Andante. ♩=116.
BARITONE SOLO.
And out of these a chant for the sailors of all nations,
And out of these a chant for the sai-lors of all na-tions,
M
Animando.
Fit-ful, like a

N
surge.
Fit - ful, like a surge, like a
Fit - ful, like a surge, like a
Fit - ful, like a surge, like a
Fit - ful, like a surge,
p agitato
m. s.
N
Of sea - cap-tains young or old, and the mates, and of
surge, fit - - - - - - ful,
surge, fit - - - - - - ful,
surge, fit - - - - -ful, like a
like a
m. d.

O
all in-trep-id sai - lors,
p
f
of all in - trep - id sai - lors, of
fp
surge
of all
of
O
p agitato
Of the few, ve - ry choice,
all in - trep - id
all in - trep - id
in - trep - id
all in - trep - id

molto allargando
tac - i-turn, whom fate can nev - er sur - prise nor
sail - - - - ors,
sail - - - - ors,
sail - - - - ors,
sail - - - - ors,
molto allargando
marcato
ff
p subito
P
Più mosso.
death dis - may,
whom fate can nev - er sur - prise nor death dis - may,
whom fate can nev - er sur - prise nor death dis - may,
whom fate can nev - er sur - prise nor death dis - may,
whom fate can nev - er sur - prise nor death dis - may,
P
Più mosso.

Picked spar-ing-ly with-out noise by thee old o-cean,
simile
Q
Picked spar-ing-ly with-out noise by thee old o-cean, cho-sen by thee,
Picked spar-ing-ly with-out noise by thee old o-cean, cho-sen by thee,
Picked spar-ing-ly with-out noise by thee old o-cean, cho-sen by thee,
Picked spar-ing-ly with-out noise by thee old o-cean, cho-sen by thee,
Q
Thou sea that pick-est and cull-est the race in time, and u-
Thou
Thou sea, thou that pick-est, thou that cull-est,
Thou that pick-est, cull-est
Thou sea, thou that pick-est, thou that cull-est
subito
agitato

R
allargando
a tempo
-nit - cresc. - - - - - est the na - tions, Suck - led by
sea,
p cresc.
allargando.
a tempo.
Thou that u - nit-est the na-tions,
p cresc.
allargando.
a tempo.
Thou that u - nit-est the na-tions,
p cresc.
allargando.
a tempo.
Thou that u - nit-est the na-tions,
R
allargando
a tempo
f marc.
thee, old hus-ky nurse, em - bod-y-ing thee,
S molto allargando
In - do - mit - a - ble, untamed as thee.
un - tamed as
un - tamed as
un - tamed as
un - tamed as
S molto allargando
p cresc.
colla voce

Moderato. ♩= 80.
SOPRANO SOLO.
quasi recit.
Flaunt out O sea your separate flags of
thee
thee.
thee.
thee.
Moderato. ♩= 80.
ff
p
na-tions!
ff
Flaunt out O sea your separate flags of
ff
Flaunt out O sea your separate flags of
ff
Flaunt out O sea your separate flags of
ff
Flaunt out O sea your separate flags of
f

T
molto stringendo.
na-tions!
na-tions!
na-tions!
na-tions!
T
molto stringendo.
a tempo.
SOPRANO SOLO.
Flaunt out vi-si-ble as ev-er the va-ri-ous flags and ship-signals!
U
Flaunt out vi-si-ble as ev-er the va-ri-ous flags and ship-signals!
Flaunt out vi-si-ble as ev-er the va-ri-ous flags and ship-signals!
Flaunt out vi-si-ble as ev-er the va-ri-ous flags and ship-signals!
Flaunt out vi-si-ble as ev-er the va-ri-ous flags and ship-signals!
U

stringendo.
molto rall.
SOPRANO SOLO.
Molto tranquillo. ♩ = 72.
p dolce.
But do you reserve es - pe - ciall - y for your - self and for the soul of man
p
p dolce.
And for the soul of man
p dolce e cantabile.
But do

for the soul of
the soul of man
you re-serve es - pe-ciall - y for your-self
p dolce.
But do you re-serve
3
3
(6)
man
p cresc.
one flag a -
cresc.
one flag a - - bove all the
cresc.
and for the soul of man one flag
cresc.
for the soul of man
cresc.

one flag
-bove all the rest,
rest, all the rest,
one flag a - bove all the
one flag a - bove all
Poco animando.
a - bove all the rest
Poco animando.
a
Poco animando.
a wov - - - - - - - en
Poco animando. mp cantabile.
rest, a spi - ri - tu - al wov - en sig - nal for all na - - tions,
Poco animando.
p cantabile.
the rest, a spi - ri - tu - al,
Poco animando.

one flag a-
cresc.
espr.
wov-en sig - - nal for all na-tions a
sig - nal for all
sig - nal for all na - tions, all na - - - -
p cantabile.
a spi-ri-tu-al woven sig - nal for all na - tions,
cresc.
wov-en sig - nal for all na - tions, one flag a - bove all the
cresc.
- bove all the rest, a wov-en sig - nal for
cresc.
wov-en sig - nal for all na - - tions, one flag a -
mf cresc.
- tions, a wov - en
cresc.
all na - - tions, for all
tok - - en for all
rest, a tok - - en for all

V
all nations,
-bove all the rest,
emblem of man
sig - - - nal,
em - blem of man
f
nations, em - blem of man e - late a-bove death,
V
f marcato
Andante. ♩= 72.
ff
Tok - en of all brave cap-tains
(Em - blem)
e - late a - bove death,
e - late a-bove death,
em-blem of man e - late a-bove death,
e - late a-bove death,
em-blem of man e - late a - bove death,
Andante. ♩= 72.

W
CHORUS.
— and of all in - tre - pid sai-lors and mates,
Alti.
mf molto espr.
Tok - en of all brave
W espr.
cap - tains and of all in - tre-pid sai-lors and mates, And of all that went
Sopr.
(only half to sing)
Tok - en of all brave cap - tains and of
CHORUS.
down do-ing their du - - - - - - ty,
mf espr.
Re-min-is - cent of
all in - - tre - - pid sai-lors and mates, And all that went
them, twined from all in - tre - - - pid

down do-ing their du - ty, Re-min-is - cent of them, twined
cap - - - tains twined from all
(only half to sing)
p
Tok - en of all brave cap-tains, and of all in - tre - pid
from all in - tre - - - - - - - pid
cap - tains young or old, Tok - en of
sailors and mates, and all that went down do-ing their du - ty, twined
Tutti. divisi.
Tutti. p espr.
Tok - en of all brave cap - tains,
X
p

Tutti.
espr.
cap - tains and all that went down
all brave cap - - - tains
Tutti.
from all in - trep - - id cap - tains,
rem - in - is - cent of them,
doing their du - - - - - - ty, re-min -
Re-min-is - cent of them,
all brave unis.
tok - en of all brave cap - -
tok - en of all in - trep - id
Re-min-is - cent of them, twined from all in - trep - id
tok - en of all brave cap - - -

-is - centof them, twined from all in - trep - - - - id cap - tains
- - tains, and all in - trep - - id sai - - - - - -
mf
sai - lors all in - trep - id sai-lors and mates tok - en of
mf
- - - - - - - - - tains, tok - en of all
mf
tok - - - - - - en,
cresc.
tok - - -
mf
- - - lors, all sai - - - - - - - - lors and
cresc.
all to - en of all
— in - trep - id sai - lorsand mates,
cresc.

Y
ff
- - en of all brave cap - tains and of all
mates, all brave cap - - - tains and of
cresc.
of all that went down do - - -
cresc.
tok - en of all all of all in -
Y
8
molto allargando
dim.
in - tre - pid sai-lors and mates
molto allargando
ff dim.
all in - - tre - - - pid sai - lors and
molto allargando
ff dim.
- - - - - - ing their du - - - ty,
molto allargando
ff dim.
tre - - - - - - - pid sai - - - - - lors and
molto allargando.
8
ff
legato

Poco meno mosso.
p
mates.
tranquillo
p espr.
Tok - en of all that went down
p
mates.
Poco meno mosso.
p tranquillo
p espr.
tok - en of
do-ing their du - - - ty.
p espr.
tok - en of all that went down do - ing their du - - ty,

all that went down do - ing their du - - - ty,
p espr.
Re-min-is-cent of them, twined from all in - tre - pid cap - tains.
p espr.
Re-min-is-cent of them, twined from all, young or old.
p
young or old.
Z
p
p espr.
Re-min-is-cent of them, twined from all in - tre - pid cap-tains
Ancora più tranquillo.
pp
young or
pp

old,
pp
young or old,
p
em - blem of
pp
young or old,
Animato. (𝅗𝅥 = ♩ of the preceding bar.)
f risoluto
em - blem of man e-late a-bove
(𝅗𝅥 = ♩)
f
em - blem
(𝅗𝅥 = ♩) poco f risoluto
(𝅗𝅥 = ♩) man e-late a-bove death e - late a - bove death,
f
em - blem
Animato. (𝅗𝅥 = ♩ of the preceding bar.)
mf
mf marcato
f marcato
Aa
death a - bove death e - late a - bove death,
f risoluto
em - blem of man e - late a-bove death a - bove
f risoluto
em - blem of man e - late a-bove death a - bove
f risoluto
em - blem of man e-late a-bove death a - bove death,
Aa
f

f
e - late a-bove death,
ff
em -
death
f
e - late a - bove death
ff
em - blem of
death
f
e - late a - bove death
em - - blem of man
f
em - blem of man
ff
em - blem of man e
sempre marcato
Bb
- blem of man e - late a-bove death,
man e - late a-bove death e-late a-bove death, a - bove
e - late a-bove death a-bove death, of man e-late a-bove
-late a-bove death em - blem of man e - - late a - bove
Bb
emblem of man e - late a - bove
death, of man e - late a - bove death of man e - late a - bove
death, a - bove death, em-blem of man e - late a-bove
death, em-blem of man of man e - late a - bove death,

Ancora più mosso.
death,
death,
death
più mosso.
ff
Em - blem of man e - late a - bove
Ancora più mosso.
ff sempre cresc.
m.d.
ff
em - blem of man e - late a - bove
death,
ff
em - blem of man e - late a - bove death,
ff
em - blem of man e - late a - bove death,
death,
ff
em - blem of
ff
em - blem of
Cc

e - late
a-bove death,
a-bove
man e - late
death,
Tempo del principio. (♩ = 𝅗𝅥 of preceding bar)
dim.
fff
pp

BARITONE SOLO
largamente.
f
largamente.
cantabile.
Dd
pen - nant un - i - ver - - sal,
ff
A pennant un-i-ver - - sal,
A pennant un-i-ver - - sal,
A pennant un-i-ver - - sal,
A pennant un-i-ver - - sal,
Dd

sub - tly wav - ing all time o'er
all brave sail - - - - - - ors,
a pen - nant un - i -
a pen - nant un - i -
a pen - nant un - i -
a pen - nant un - i -

a pennant un-i-ver - - - sal,
-ver - - sal,
sub - tly
-ver - - sal,
sub - - - - tly
sub - tly
div.
-ver - - sal,
sub - - - - tly
-ver - - sal,
sub - - - - tly
wav - ing all time, o'er all brave
wav - - - - - ing o'er all brave
wav - ing all time,
wav - - - - - ing o'er all brave
wav - - - - - ing o'er all brave

BARITONE SOLO
A pen - nant un - i - ver - - sal,
sail - ors,
sail - ors,
sail - ors,
sail - ors,
p
3
— sub - tly wav - - - - ing all
mf
f
a
a pen - nant un - i - ver -
a
a pen - nant un - i - ver -
6
mf
6

time,
pen - - nant un - i - ver - - - sal, sub - tly wav - - - ing
- - sal, sub - tly wav - ing all time, o'er all brave
pen - nant un - - i - ver - - - sal, sub - tly wav - - - ing
- - sal, sub - tly wav - ing all time, o'er all brave
Ee
animando.
SOPRANO SOLO
f
a pen - nant un - i -
BARITONE SOLO
o'er all brave sail - - - - ors,
all time,
sail-ors,
all time,
Ee
sail - - ors,
animando.
p

ver - - sal, a pen-nant un - i -
mf
o'er all brave sail - - - - - ors,
mf
o'er all brave sail - - - - - ors,
mf
o'er all brave sail - - - - - ors,
mf
o'er all brave sail - - - - - ors,
molto allargando.
- ver - - - - - - - - - - - - - - sal,
f cresc.
molto allarg.
o'er all brave sail - - - - - ors,
mf cresc.
molto allarg.
o'er all brave sail - - - ors,
mf cresc.
molto allarg.
o'er all brave sail - - ors,
mf cresc.
molto allarg.
o'er all brave sail - - - - ors,
mf cresc.
molto allarg.
o'er all brave sail - - - - - ors,
molto allargando.
mf

Tempo del principio, ma molto largamente.
Ff
ff
one flag one flag a-
one flag one flag a-
one flag one flag a-
one flag one flag a-
one flag one flag a-
one flag one flag a-
Tempo del principio, ma molto largamente.
Ff
ff
-bove all the rest, one flag one flag
-bove all the rest, one flag a-bove all the
-bove all the rest, one flag a-bove all the
-bove all the rest, one flag a-bove all the
-bove all the rest, one flag a-bove all the
-bove all the rest, one flag one
fff

Gg
a - bove all the rest,
rest,
p misterioso
rest,
Be - hold, the sea it -
rest,
rest,
flag
Gg
p
pp
p misterioso
Soprano Solo.
p quasi recit.
Be - hold, the
- self,
p misterioso
Be - hold, the sea it - self,
pp
p misterioso
pp

sea it-self, and on its lim-it-less, heav-ing breast the
pp
Hh Poco più mosso.
Soprano Solo.
ships.
Baritone Solo.
p tranquillo
All seas, all ships all seas,
CHORUS.
Sopr. I.II.
All seas, all ships.
All seas, all ships.
Alti. I.II.
All brave sail-ors all seas,
All seas, all seas,
Ten I.II.
O'er all brave sail-ors, all seas
O'er all seas all ships o'er
Bassi. I.II.
One flag a-bove all the
One flag a-bove all the
Hh Poco più mosso.
pp

*) *Note.* Only a few Basses (about 1/6th) to sing the first bass.

No. 2. On the Beach at Night alone.

C
pp
As the old mo - ther sways her to and fro sing-ing her husk - y song,
pp
As the old
ppp
pp
moth - er sways her to and fro sing-ing her husk - y song,
As I
cantando
watch the bright stars shin - - - - - - - ing,
pp
As I
D
watch the bright stars shin - ing,
f
p

pp
I think a thought of the clef of the u-ni-ver-ses and of the
pp
E
fu - ture
ppp
pp
ppp
pochettino rall.
pp
Poco meno mosso.
p dolce.
BARITONE SOLO
F
p dolce
SEMI CHORUS.
A vast si - mil - i-tude in - ter - locks
SOPR.
pp
A vast si -
ALTI.
pp
A vast si - mil - i -
TEN.
pp
A vast si -
BASSI.
pp
A vast si - mil - i - tude
F

G
p
all,
All dis-tances of
pp
-mil-i-tude
All
pp
-tude
All dis-tan-ces
-mil-i-tude in-ter-locks all,
G
mp
space how-ev-er wide,
All
space how-ev-er wide,
space how-ev-er wide,
how-ev-er wide,
pp
all space how-ev-er wide,
pp
all space how-ev-er

H Poco animando.
dis - tan-ces of time, All souls,
All dis - tan-ces of time,
All time, All souls,
wide All souls,
Poco animando.
pp
mf marcato
Largamente. a tempo.
Largamente.
All souls, all liv - ing bod-ies
all liv - ing bod-ies
All souls, all liv - ing bod-ies
all liv - ing bod-ies
Largamente.
a tempo.

Poco animando. .
p
All souls,— all liv - - ing bod - ies
p
All souls, all
p
All souls, all living
Poco animando.
p
mp
though they be
p
All souls, all liv - ing bod - - - - - - - ies
p
All——— souls, all liv- ing bod - - - - - ies
liv - ing bod - - - ies
p
bod-ies all— liv - ing bod - ies

ev - er so dif - ferent,
p cresc.
dim.
All souls, all liv - ing
though they be ev - er so dif -
though they be ev - er so dif -
All souls, all liv - ing
cresc.
K Ancora più mosso.
mf solenne.
All na - tions, all i - den - ti - ties,
bod - ies,
All na - tions, all i -
- ferent,
All na - tions, all i -
bod - ies,
All na - tions, all i -
Ancora più mosso.
p

L
pp cresc.
-den-ti-ties that have ex-ist - ed___ or may ex - ist,___ All lives and
pp cresc.
-den-ti-ties that have ex-ist - ed___ or may ex - ist,___ All lives and
pp cresc.
-den-ti-ties that have ex-ist - ed___ or may ex - ist,___ All lives and
pp cresc.
-den-ti-ties that have ex-ist - ed___ or may ex - ist,___ All lives and
L
p
cresc.
p cresc.
All lives and deaths, all of the past pres - ent, fu - ture,
f
deaths, all of the past pres - ent, fu - ture,
f
deaths, all of the past pres - ent, fu - ture,
f
deaths, all of the past pres - ent, fu - ture,
f
deaths, all of the past pres - ent, fu - ture,
f

FULL CHORUS.
M
This vast si-mil-i-tude spans them, and al-ways has spanned,
allargando
a tempo
fff tutta forza
allarg.
And shall for ev-er span them, and shall com-pact-ly hold and en-
close them.
O
p molto cresc.
ff pesante

Tempo del principio.
P
mf
f
p
mf
pp
ppp
BARITONE SOLO.
p misterioso
On the beach at night a - lone,
at night a - lone.
p cantando
Q misterioso
pp
p
più p
R molto tranquillo.
pp
ppp
smorzando
pppp

Nº 3. Scherzo.- The Waves.

SOPR.
ALTI.
TEN.
BASS.
Below a myriad myriad waves hastening,
After the sea - ship,
molto cresc.
marc. cresc.
f brillante
After the whistling winds,
Below, a
p cresc.
B

p cresc.
Be - low, a
- low, a my - riad waves hast - en - ing, hast - en - ing,
my - riad my - riad waves hast - en - ing, hast - en - ing,
my - riad my - riad waves hast - en - ing, hast - en - ing,
poco f
my - riad waves hast - en - ing, lift - ing up
hast - en - ing, hast - en - ing,
poco f
hast - en - ing, lift - ing up
hast - en - ing,
Pic.
poco f
C
f
their necks,
poco f
lift - ing up
f
lift - ing up their necks,
poco f
their necks,
lift - ing up
f
lift - ing up their necks,
C
f
poco f

their necks,
lift-ing up their necks,
their necks,
lift-ing up their necks,
Animando. 𝅗𝅥 = 164.
Tend-ing in cease - less
Animando.
Tend-ing in cease - less
mf Animando.
Tend-ing in cease - less flow toward the
mf Animando.
Tend-ing in cease - less flow toward the
Animando. 𝅗𝅥 = 164.
flow toward the track of the ship,
flow toward the track of the ship,
track of the ship,
poco f
Af-ter the
track of the ship,
poco f
Af-ter the
D
D

poco f
After the whistling winds,
poco f
After the whistling winds,
sea - ship,
After the whistling winds,
sea - ship,
After the whist ling winds,
m.s.
mf
Waves of the
mf
Waves of the
mf
Waves of the o - cean
mf
Waves of the o - cean
p
E
o - cean bub - bling and gurg - ling,
o - cean bub - bling and gurg - ling, blithe - ly
bub - bling and gurg - ling, blithe - ly
bub - bling and gurg - ling, blithe - ly
E
mf

f
ff
blithe - - ly pry - - - - - - - - - - - - ing,
pry - - - ing,
pry ing,
pry - - - - ing,
ff
dim.
p
F Ancora animando.
p molto cresc.
ff
Waves, un - - - du - lat - ing
Waves,
Waves,
Waves,
F Ancora animando.
p molto cresc.
ff

waves
p molto cresc.
Waves
p molto cresc.
Waves
f marc.
p molto cresc.
f
p
ff
G
Waves, un - - du-la-ting waves,
Waves,
ff
f marc.
p cantabile e legato
liqu - - id, un - ev - en,
p subito
p

em - - - u - lous waves,
p cantabile e legato
liqu - - - - id, un - - ev - - - en, em - - - - - u - lous
p
em - - - u - lous waves,
p
em - - - u - lous waves,
H
p cresc.
waves, To - ward that whirl - - - - - ing
p cresc.
To - ward that whirl - - - - - ing
p cresc.
mf cresc.
f dim.
To - ward that whirl - - - - ing cur - - rent,
mf cresc.
To - ward that whirl - - - - ing cur - - rent,
cur - rent,
cur - rent,
f dim.

I
f brillante
laugh - ing and buoy - ant
f brillante
laugh - ing and buoy - ant
f brillante
laugh - ing and buoy - ant
f cresc.
laugh - ing and
f brillante
laugh - ing and buoy - ant
f cresc.
laugh - ing and buoy - -
ff
f cresc.
laugh - ing and buoy - - - - - - - ant with
f cresc.
laugh - ing and buoy - - - - - - - - ant with
buoy - - - ant buoy - - - - - - - - ant with
- ant buoy - - - - - - - - - - ant with

ff
curves,
Allargando.
f Largamente.
K
Where the great ves - sel sail - ing, sail - - - - - - ing and
Where the great ves - sel sail ing and
Where the great ves - sel sail - ing, Where the great ves - sel sail ing and
Where the great ves - sel sail ing and
Largamente.
tack-ing dis - placed the sur-face,
p legato
Lar-ger and small - er

cresc.
waves in the spread of the o - cean yearn-ful - ly flow - - - - - -
waves in the spread of the o - cean yearn-ful - ly flow - - - - -
f
- - - - ing, The wake of the sea - ship af - ter she
ff
Più mosso.
pass - es, af - ter she pass - - - - - - - - es,
Più mosso.

M
ff brillante
flash - ing and frol - ics-some un - der the sun,
ff brillante
flash - ing and frol - ics-some un - der the sun,
ff brillante
flash - ing and frol - ics-some un der the sun,
ff brillante
flash - ing and frol - ics-so un - der the sun,
M
ff
3
3
ff
flash - ing and frol - ics-some un - der the sun,
ff
flash - ing and frol - ics-some un - der the sun,
ff
flash - ing and frol - ics-some un - der the sun,
ff
flash - ing and frol - ics-some un - der the sun,
N
N
3
3
sempre ff

TROMBE.
COR.
O
dim.
p
TEN.
BASSI.
Ancora animando.
mp marc.
A mot - ley pro-
animando
Ancora animando.
P
A mot - ley pro - ces - sion
-ces - sion
with many a
mf

mp
f fp molto cresc. f
with man - y a fleck of foam,
fleck of foam, of foam,
fleck of foam, of foam,
fleck of foam, of foam,
p cresc.
Q
p cresc.
of foam and man - y frag-ments,
of foam and man - y frag-ments,
of foam and man - y frag-ments,
of foam and man - y frag-ments,
ff p molto cresc. ff
ff f
Af-ter the sea - ship, af-ter the whist - ling
Af-ter the sea - ship, af-ter the whist - ling
Af-ter the sea - ship, af-ter the whist - ling
Af-ter the sea - ship, af-ter the whist - ling

R Più animando. (beat 1 in the bar)
winds,
winds,
winds,
winds,
R Più animando. (beat 1 in the bar)
p
8
8
p
S

★*Note* The chorus parts may be omitted from letter T to two bars after U.

ff foam — f and man - y frag - - ments,

ff foam ff and man - y ff frag - - - - ments,

f and man - y frag - - ments,

ff and man - y ff frag - - - - ments,

f cresc. — f cresc. — ff

fff

ff dim. — f dim. — mf dim.

mp — p dim. — ppp

Tempo del principio.
p ma risoluto
After the sea-ship,
after the whistling winds,
Tempo del principio.
ppp
f
p
fp
mf
W
mp
fp subito

poco f
After the white-gray sails taut to their
f p cresc.
risoluto
After the white-gray sails taut to their spars and ropes,
spars and ropes,
Below, a
mp cresc.
Below, a myriad myriad waves
myriad myriad waves hastening
fp

mf
hast - en - ing,
mf cresc.
lift - ing up their
mf
hast - en - ing,
mf cresc.
lift - ing up their
mf cresc.
lift - ing up their necks,
mf cresc.
lift - ing up their necks,
mf cresc.
Y
f
necks,
f
lift-ing up their necks,
ff
f
necks,
f
lift-ing up their necks,
ff
f
lift-ing up their necks,
ff
lift-ing up their necks,
Y
f
ff marc.

Z
Largamente.
in the wake fol - - lowing,
in the wake fol - - lowing, fol - lowing,
in the wake fol - lowing, fol - p - - lowing,
Fol-low-ing the state-ly and ra - pid ship,
fol - - - - lowing, fol - lowing,
ff marc.
p legato
cresc.
mf
f
Aa
fol - lowing. A mot - ley pro - ces - sion with man - y a
A mot - ley pro - ces - sion with man - y a

Più mosso.
Bb
ff dim.
fleck of foam and man-y frag - - - - - - - - ments,
più mosso.
fleck of foam and man-y frag - - - - - - - - ments,
fleck of foam and man-y frag - - - - - - - - ments,
fleck of foam and man-y frag - - - - - - - - ments,
Più mosso.
Eb
p
mp
A mot - ley pro - ces - sion
mf
A mot - ley pro -
A mot-ley pro - ces - sion
A mot-ley pro - ces - sion

Cc
-ces - sion
poco f
with many a fleck of foam and many
poco f
with many a fleck of foam and many
poco f
with man-y a fleck of foam
poco f
with man-y a fleck of foam
Cc
f
poco stringendo.
f
frag-ments Fol-lowing the state-ly and ra - pid ship,
Dd Poco piú mosso.
string.
f
frag-ments Fol-lowing the state-ly and ra - pid ship,
più mosso.
string.
f
string. Fol-lowing the state - - - ly and ra - pid ship,
più mosso.
f
Fol-lowing the state - - - ly and ra - pid ship,
più mosso.
poco stringendo.
Dd Poco piú mosso.
ff
ff
in the wake fol-low-ing,
ff
in the wake fol-low-ing,
ff
in the wake fol-low-ing,
ff
in the wake fol-low-ing,
ff

Ee
ff
fol - lowing,
fol - lowing,
fol - lowing,
fol - lowing,
Ee
Ped.
fol - lowing,
fol - lowing,
fol - lowing,
fol - lowing,
Ped.
fol - - - lowing.
fol - - - lowing.
fol - - - lowing.
fol - - - lowing.

Nº 4. The Explorers.

mf
Cov-ered all o-ver with vi-si-ble power and beau - - - - - -
o - - - ver with power and
- - - - ty,
sempre legato.
mf
- - ty, Al-ter-nate light and day and the
f
beau - ty, Al - ter - nate light and day
Al - ter - nate light and day
Al-ter-nate light and day al - ter - nate light and day and the
pp
teem-ing spi-rit-u-al dark - ness
A
Unspeakable high pro-ces-sions
and the teem-ing spi-rit-u-al dark - ness, Un-speakable
and the teem - ing spi-rit-u-al dark - ness, Un - speakable
teem-ing spi-rit-u-al dark - ness, Unspeak-able high pro-ces - sions

p
of sun and moon
pp
and count - less
p
high pro - ces - sions of sun and moon
p
pp
high pro - ces - sions of sun and moon
and count - less
p
of sun and moon
p
stars a - bove,
p
stars a - bove,
Be - low,
p
and count-less stars a - bove,
Be - low,
p
stars a - bove,
Be - low, the
p
Be-low, the man - i-fold
the grass and wa - ters,
mf parlando.
With in - scrut - a-ble
the man-i-fold grass and wa - ters,
mf parlando.
With in - scrut - a-ble
grass and wa - ters,
mf parlando.
With in - scrut - a-ble
grass and wa - ters,
mf parlando.
With in - scrut - a-ble

pur - - pose, some hid - - - den prophetic in - ten - tion,
pur - - pose, some hid - - - den prophetic in - ten - tion,
pur - - pose, some hid - - - den prophetic in - ten - tion,
pur - - pose, some hid - - - den prophetic in - ten - tion,
mf
f
B
p
pp
Now first it seems my thoughts be-gin to span thee.
Now first it seems my thoughts be-gin to span thee.
Now first it seems my thoughts be-gin to span thee.
Now first it seems my thoughts be-gin to span thee.
B

Andante con moto. 𝅗𝅥=48
TENORI.
pp misterioso
Down from the
BASSI.
pp misterioso
Down from the
Andante con moto. 𝅗𝅥=48
pp
p
gar - dens of As - ia des - cend - ing. Ad - am and Eve ap -
gar - dens of As - ia des cend - ing, Ad - am and Eve ap -
- pear, then their my - riad pro - ge - ny af - - ter them,
- pear, then their my - riad pro - ge - ny af - - ter them,
C
C
mf
Wand - er - ing,
mf
Wand - er - ing,
p
mf

yearn - ing, with rest-less ex - plor -
yearn - ing with rest-less ex - plor - a - tions,
p
a - - tions,
With quest-ion-ings,
With quest-ion-ings,
mp
mf
D
form - less,
fev - er-ish,
baf - fled,
fev - er-ish,
f
with never - hap - py hearts,
largamente
with ne-ver-hap - - py
p dim
largamente

*) *Note.* To ensure correct intonation the opening chord may be accompanied by a harmonium, which may play the chord two bars before the chorus enters

TENOR.
mf
Ah who shall soothe these fev - er-ish child - ren? Who
BASS.
Ah who shall soothe these fev - er-ish child - ren? Who
p pesante
fp
jus - ti-fy these rest less ex-plor - a - tions? Who speak the se - cret of the im-
jus - ti-fy these rest less ex-plor - a - tions? Who speak the se - cret of the im-
F
f
mf cresc.
p
SOPRANI.
ppp
Where fore un - sat is-fied
SEMICHORUS.
ALTI.
pp
Where fore un - sat - is-fied
pass - - - - - - ive earth?
pass - - - - - - ive earth?
pp
ppp

whith - - - - er O mock - ing life?
soul? whith - - er O mock - ing life?
Tempo I.
SOPRANO. (Tutti.)
ALTO. (Tutti.)
TENORI.
BASSI.
Yet soul be sure the first in - tent re - mains, and
Tempo I.
Yet soul be sure the first in - tent re -
Yet soul be sure the first in - tent re -
shall be car - ried out and shall be car - - ried out,

G
mf
Yet soul be sure the first in - tent re-mains,
-mains, and shall be car - ried out,
Per-hapse-ven now the
-mains, and shall be car - ried out,
Per-hapse-ven now the
Per-hapse-ven now the
G
mf
time has ar - rived
af - ter the seas
time has ar - rived
af - ter the seas
time has ar - rived
time has ar - rived
are all crossed
are all crossed
Af - ter the great cap-tains have ac -
Af - ter the great cap-tains have ac -
8

animando
f
Af - ter the nob - le in - ven - tors,
-com-plished their work,
f marc.
H
Animato
ff
Fin - - al - ly
fin - - al - ly
Animato.

Largamente.
shall come the po - - - - et
Largamente.
a tempo
wor-thy that name, The true son of
a tempo.
God shall come sing - - - - - ing
m. s.

- - - - - - - - - - - ing sing - - - -
sing - - - - - - ing,
- ing sing - - - - - - - ing sing - - - - - ing,
sing - - - - - - - - - - - ing,
- ing his songs, sing - - ing sing - - - - - ing, sing - - -
sing - ing, sing - ing his songs, sing - - - - ing, sing - -
sing - ing, sing - ing his songs, sing - - - - - ing, sing - - -
sing - ing, singing his songs, sing - - - - ing, sing - - - - - ing,
- - ing, sing - - ingsinging his songs sing - ing sing -
- - ing, singing his songs, sing - ing sing -
- ing, sing - ing singing his songs, sing - ing sing -
sing - ing, sing - ing singing his songs, sing - ing sing -
K

fff
ing, sing - - - - - ing, sing - ing sing - - - - ing his
fff
- ing, sing - - - - - ing, sing - ing sing - - - - ing his
fff
- ing, sing - - - - - ing, sing - ing sing - - - - ing his
fff
- ing, sing - - - - - ing, sing - ing sing - - - - ing his
fff
Allegro animato. ♩ = 140.
songs.
songs.
songs.
songs.
Allegro animato. ♩ = 140.
ff
f

L

f *f* *dim.* *f* *p*

BARITONE SOLO.

♩ = ♩ *f appassionato.* *f* *p*

O we can wait no long - er, We too take ship O— soul, Joy - ous we too launch out on track - less

SOPRANO SOLO.
f appassionato.
O we can wait no long-er, Joy - - - - - - ous we too launch
seas, Joy - - - - ous we too launch out on trackless
out on trackless seas,
seas,
mf
Fear - less for un - known
shores on waves of ec-stasy to sail,
mf
Fear - less for un-known shores on waves of ec-sta-sy to
Animato.
f
ff
A - mid the waft - - ing winds,
ff
sail, A - mid the waft - - ing winds,
Animato.
ff

M
mf
cresc.
Thou pressing me to thee, Thou pressing
mf
O soul
p
me to thee,
f
I thee to me
O soul thou pressing me
f
f
I thee to me,
to thee, O soul, thou pressing me to thee,
f
Car - - - ol - ing free,
f
Car - - - ol - ing free,

sing - - - - ing our song of
sing - - - - ing our song of
God,
p cresc.
Chant - ing our
God,
p cresc.
chant of pleas - ant ex - plo -
p cresc.
Chant - - - - - ing our chant of ex - plo -
ra - - - - - tion
D f
chant - - - - - - - - -
ra - - - - - tion
f
chant - - - - - - - - -
f

p smorzando.
- - - ing our chant of pleasant ex - - - - plo -
smorzando.
p
- - - ing our chant of
p smorzando.
poco rall.
- ra - tion.
pleasant explo - ra - - tion.
poco rall.
smorzando.
Andante tranquillo. ♩ = 60
p dolce.
Tempo rubato.
pp
m. s.
pp
a tempo.
BARITONE SOLO.
P
p tranquillo.
O soul thou pleas - est me, I thee,
pp

SOPRANO SOLO
p molto tranquillo.
Sail-ing these seas or on the hills,
Thoughts,
Sail-ing these seas,
or wak - ing in the night
p
si - lent thoughts,
of Time and Space
Thoughts, si - lent thoughts, of Time and
m. s.
and Death, like wa - ters flow-ing,
pp
Space and Death, like wa - ters flowing,
pp
pp
pp
Bear me in - deed as through reg - - - - - ions in-fin-ite
Q
Bear me in - deed as through reg - - - - ions in-fin-ite

* *Note* A 'cut' may be made from this place to the mark ⊕ on page 106. The solo voices will sing the music of the bar above marked *

simile.
R SOPRANO SOLO.
O thou trans - cend - - ent,
BARITONE SOLO.
O thou trans - cend - - ent,
R
CHORUS.
SOPR.
O thou trans - cend - - ent,
ALTI.
O thou trans - cend - - ent,
TEN.
O thou trans - cend - - ent,
BASS.
O thou trans - cend - - ent,

SOPRANO SOLO.
Name - less, the fi - bre and the breath,
BARITONE SOLO.
Name - less, the fi - bre and the breath,
Name - less, the fi - bre and the
Name - less, the fi - bre and the
Name - less, the fi - bre and the
Name - less, the fi - bre and the
Light of the light, shed - ding forth un - i - ver - ses,
Light of the light, shed - ding forth un - i - ver - ses,
breath, Light of the light, shed -
breath, Light of the light, shed -
breath, Light of the light, shed -
breath, Light of the light, shed -

ff
thou centre of them.
ff
thou centre of them.
f
- ding forth un - i - ver - ses, thou centre of them.
- ding forth un - i - ver - ses, thou centre of them.
- ding forth un - i - ver - ses, thou centre of them.
- ding forth un - i - ver - ses, thou centre of them.
cresc.
S
p
Swiftly I shrivel
pp

BARITONE SOLO.
— at the thought of God,
At na - ture
and its won - ders
— Time and Space and Death, —
cantabile.
dolce.
But that I, turn - ing,
pp tranquillo.
— call to thee O Soul, thou act - - ual me,
And
lo, thou gent - ly — mas - terest the orbs,
T
thou mat est Time,
smil - est con -
p

◆ End of optional 'cut'

U
SOPRANO SOLO.
A-way
BARITONE SOLO.
Away O soul!
A-way
A-way
A-way
A-way
U
away
away
away
O soul!

f marc.
hoist instantly the anchor.
f
a - way
away
away O soul!
away
away
away
away O soul!
ff marc.
Cut the hawsers
away
ff

V
away O soul!
a-way
a-way
away
V
a-way O soul!
a-way O soul!
a-way
haul
a-way O soul!
a-way
out-
haul out,
haul out-
away O soul!
shake out ev-'ry sail!
shake out ev'ry sail!
a-
haul out,
haul out,-
haul
-way O soul!
a-way O soul!
away a-

-way a-way, a-way, a-
out, a-way, a-way a-way, a
-way, a-way, shake out, shake out ev-ry
marcato.
shake out ev'ry sail,
-way, a-way O soul!
-way O soul!
sail! a-way O soul!
strepitoso.

Più lento ♩=100
W
allarg.
affrett.
Sail
forth
ff
p
Ped.
allarg.
a tempo affrett.

allarg.
a tempo.
affrett.
steer for the deep waters on - - - - ly.
allarg.
a tempo
affrett.
steer for the deep waters deep wa-ters on - - - - ly.
allarg.
a tempo
affrett.
steer for the deep wa-ters on - ly.
allarg.
a tempo
affrett.
steer for the deep wa-ters on - ly.
allarg.
a tempo.
affrett.
Allegro agitato. = 90
SOPRANO SOLO.
Reck - less O soul, ex - plor - - - - ing, I with thee, and
BARITONE SOLO.
Reck - less O soul, ex - plor - - ing,
Allegro agitato. = 90

★ *Note* The chorus parts between ★ and ✦ on page 114 may be omitted.

✦ Chorus obbligato from here.

più f
I with thee, and thou with me, Sail forth
ff
più f
I with thee, and thou with me, Sail forth
ff
forth steer for the deep waters on
f
forth steer for the deep waters on
f
forth steer for the deep waters on
f
forth steer for the deep waters on
f
ff dim.
steer for the deep waters on - ly,
Animato.
steer for the deep waters on - ly,
Animato.
ly,
p
Animato.
ly, steer for the deep wa-ters on - ly
p
f
Animato.
ly,
Animato.
ly,
p
Animato.
Animato.

mf
For we are bound where mar - i-ner has not yet dared to
pp
steer for the deep wa - ters on - - ly,
Y
mf
For we are bound where mar - i-ner
go.
pp
steer for the deep wa - ters on - ly,
pp
steer for the deep wa - ters

has not yet dared to go,
mp cresc.
Reck-less O soul, ex-plor-ing, I with
pp sostenuto
steer for the deep
pp sostenuto
steer for the
on ly.
pp
pp sostenuto
Sail forth, Sail
pp
f
And we will risk the
f
mf
thee, and thou with me, For we are bound where
wa - - - ters on - - ly,
deep wa - - - ters, steer for the
pp sostenuto
steer for the deep, the
forth, Sail forth,
Ped.

Animando
ship, ourselves and all,
Animando.
f cresc.
mar - in - er has not yet dared to go, And we will
Animando.
p
steer for the deep wa - ters on - ly
Animando.
deep wa - ters on - ly,
Animando.
p cresc.
deep wa - ters on - ly, steer for the
p
sail forth, sail forth
Animando
STRINGS.
cresc.
f
And we will risk the ship, our - selves and all.
ff
risk the ship, our - selves and all.
p cresc.
steer for the deep wa - ters on - ly,
p cresc.
steer for the deep wa - ters on - ly,
deep wa - ters, the deep wa - ters on - ly,
f
sail forth
f marcato

ff
steer for the deep wa - ters on - ly,
ff
steer for the deep wa - ters on - ly,
ff
steer for the deep wa - ters on - ly,
ff
steer for the deep wa - ters on - ly,
3
3
3
3
Z
ff
steer for the deep wa - ters on - ly
ff
steer for the deep wa - ters on - ly
ff
steer for the deep wa - ters on - ly
ff
steer for the deep wa - ters on - ly
Z
f

fff
sail
forth,
sail
forth,
sail
forth,
sail
forth,
sail
forth.
fff marc.
piccola pausa

*)Nota. The ♩ of this movement is considerably slower than the 𝅗𝅥 of the previous movement.

mf
O dar-ing joy, but safe! are they not
far - ther sail!
O dar - ing joy,
p
pp
sail forth
sail
sail forth
sail forth
sail forth
O far-ther, far - ther sail, sail forth
f
all the seas of God.
the seas of God.
forth sail forth
pp sempre tranquillo
forth sail forth O far - ther sail
sail forth
sail forth O far - ther sail!

Bb
O far-ther sail!
O far - ther sail!
O far - ther sail!
O far - - - - ther sail!
O far ther sail
O far - - - - - - ther sail!
espressivo
m. s.
Ped.
O my brave soul!
O my brave soul! O
O far-ther sail! O
O far-ther sail!
O far-ther sail!
O farther, farther, farther
legato
Due Ped.

p
pp
O far - - - - ther sail!
pp
pp
far - ther sail!
O far - - ther sail!
pp
ppp
O far - ther sail!
O
ppp
farther, farther, far-ther sail!
O
pp
ppp
O far-ther, far-ther far-ther sail!
O
ppp
sail!
O
8
Ped.
Cc
far-ther sail!
far-ther sail!
far-ther sail!
far-ther sail!
Cc
8
ppp
pppp
Ped.
Ped.
Ped.
Ped.
Ped.

www.ingramcontent.com/pod-product-compliance
Lightning Source LLC
LaVergne TN
LVHW060510100826
845148LV00006B/953

* 9 7 8 1 6 0 8 7 4 3 2 6 1 *